RACIAL JUSTICE IN AME

INDIGENOUS PEOPLES

What Is
CULTURAL APPROPRIATION?

HEATHER BRUEGL

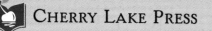
CHERRY LAKE PRESS

Published in the United States of America by Cherry Lake Publishing Group
Ann Arbor, Michigan
www.cherrylakepublishing.com

Reading Adviser: Beth Walker Gambro, MS, Ed., Reading Consultant, Yorkville, IL
Cover Art: Felicia Macheske

Produced by Focus Strategic Communications Inc.

Photo Credits: © Teko Photography, 5; © Pierre Jean Durieu/Shutterstock, 7; unknown (Republic Pictures), Public domain, via Wikimedia Commons, 9; © RGR Collection/Alamy Stock Photo, 10; Edward S. Curtis Collection, Prints and Photographs Division, Library of Congress, 11; © Moviestore Collection Ltd/Alamy Stock Photo, 12; © Teko Photography, 15; © Andrew Schwartz/Stockimo/Alamy Stock Photo, 17; © Adam McCullough/Shutterstock, 18; © miker/Shutterstock, 19; NPS, public domain, 21; © Jason Lincoln Lester/Shutterstock, 23; © LizCoughlan/Shutterstock, 24; Unknown author, Public domain, via Wikimedia Commons, 25; © Khanesuan Phonsakkhao/Shutterstock, 27; © MPH Photos/Shutterstock, 29; © Dragon Images/Shutterstock, 31

Cherry Lake Press is an imprint of Cherry Lake Publishing Group.

Library of Congress Cataloging-in-Publication Data

Names: Bruegl, Heather, author.
Title: What is cultural appropriation? / by Heather Bruegl.
Description: Ann Arbor : Cherry Lake Publishing, [2024] | Series: Racial justice in America: Indigenous peoples | Audience: Grades 7-9 | Summary: "Students will learn about cultural appropriation and its cultural and economic impact on Indigenous peoples. The Racial Justice in America: Indigenous Peoples series explores the issues specific to the Indigenous communities in the United States in a comprehensive, honest, and age-appropriate way. This series was written by Indigenous historian and public scholar Heather Bruegl, a citizen of the Oneida Nation of Wisconsin and a first-line descendant Stockbridge Munsee. The series was developed to reach children of all races and encourage them to approach race, diversity, and inclusion with open eyes and minds"— Provided by publisher.
Identifiers: LCCN 2023043604 | ISBN 9781668937983 (hardcover) | ISBN 9781668939024 (paperback) | ISBN 9781668940365 (ebook) | ISBN 9781668941713 (pdf)
Subjects: LCSH: Cultural appropriation—United States—Juvenile literature. | Indians, Treatment of—United States—Juvenile literature.
Classification: LCC E98.C88 | DDC 973.04/97—dc23/eng/20231018
LC record available at https://lccn.loc.gov/2023043604

Cherry Lake Publishing would like to acknowledge the work of the Partnership for 21st Century Learning, a Network of Battelle for Kids. Please visit Battelle for Kids online for more information.

Printed in the United States of America

Note from publisher: Websites change regularly, and their future contents are outside of our control. Supervise children when conducting any recommended online searches for extended learning opportunities.

Heather Bruegl, Oneida Nation of Wisconsin/Stockbridge-Munsee is a Madonna University graduate with a Master of Arts in U.S. History. Heather is a public historian and decolonial educator and travels frequently to present on Indigenous history, including policy and activism. In the Munsee language, Heather's name is Kiishookunkwe, meaning sunflower in full bloom.

CHAPTER 1

What Is Cultural Appropriation?

Cultural appropriation means using objects or elements of a **nondominant culture** in a way that does not respect the traditional meaning of them. Cultural appropriation does not give proper credit to members of that culture and often spreads harmful **stereotypes**. It occurs when a nondominant group's intellectual property, traditional knowledge, and cultural expression are taken without permission from the members of that culture.

Cultural appropriation can take place on a sliding scale, meaning there are different ways it can happen. All forms are harmful, but some are worse than others.

The movement to address harmful stereotypes in team names and mascots has helped to make important changes.

For example, someone may misuse the word *tribe*, while someone else may use a derogatory term, or slur, for Indigenous people. Both actions are harmful, but using a slur is worse than the other.

To understand this sliding scale, read on to explore the history of cultural appropriation in the United States.

Whenever two or more cultures meet, cultural exchange happens. Language, customs, traditions, and clothing styles may all be shared or adopted by one group or the other. There are many examples of cultural exchange that strengthen tradition and are not harmful appropriation.

The word *skunk*, for example, is an English word, but it comes from the French version of an Algonquin word. Skunks are native to North America, so Europeans did not have a name for this animal. Instead, Europeans learned a local Indigenous word to label the creature.

Indigenous artists have long created intricate art with porcupine quills. Later, Europeans introduced them to glass beads, culminating in the beadwork that is now an important part of many Indigenous traditions. Beaders create stunning and complex works of art that are often worn within the community.

Intricate beadwork is part of many nations' ceremonial regalia.

CHAPTER 2

What Is the History of Indigenous Cultural Appropriation in the U.S.?

Violence has been carried out against Indigenous people since the founding of the United States. These acts of violence include genocide, theft of land and natural resources, enslavement, forced removal, and boarding schools. These violent acts have led to the use of Indigenous culture without permission.

Indigenous imagery is evident everywhere throughout the United States today. There is a sense that anyone and everyone can use it. Members of the dominant culture take elements of Indigenous culture—their images and imagery, along with their words and phrases—and most do not face any consequences for this appropriation.

Iron Eyes Cody (left) claimed to be Indigenous. He was actually Sicilian. Roy Rogers (right) was Choctaw on his mother's side. He was a famous musician and actor who played White cowboy roles.

There are currently 574 federally recognized Indigenous nations in the United States, all with unique and distinct cultures, traditions, and ways of life. They are communities, nations, pueblos, and villages. But throughout history, Indigenous people have been portrayed in just two ways, either as good or bad Indians.

"Good Indians" were the ones who helped the Europeans. Myths retold about Squanto, Pocahontas, and Sacagawea depict a "good Indian" saving Europeans and welcoming them into their civilizations. Historical records show the real stories were much more complex.

The 1990 movie *Dances with Wolves* showed the Sioux (Lakota) to be peaceful and wise, befriending the White main character. The Pawnee, shown here, were made out to be violent and cruel.

"Good Indians" were often shown as guides to White heroes in early film and TV.

"Bad Indians" were the ones who resisted European settlement and colonization. They were portrayed in books, movies, and television shows as cruel and scary. These representations of Indigenous people only mask the realities of tribal nations struggling to maintain populations, lands, resources, and sovereignty. These representations also ignore the rich cultural history of different Indigenous nations.

The Disney animated film *Peter Pan* showed Indigenous people as both violent and silly. Disney now includes a warning before the film acknowledging its racist portrayals.

For centuries, Indigenous people in the United States have been misrepresented in many ways. Adventure stories of the "Wild West" cast Indigenous people as enemies to be controlled. White people would dress up and "play Indian," recreating false historical narratives. Indigenous speech patterns and dialects were often made fun of, and dances were fabricated that belittled their culture.

Toys, too, were used to mock Indigenous people by attempting to imitate them. Children of the dominant culture in the 1950s played "Cowboys and Indians," running around with plastic headdresses and bows and arrows. White children also dressed up as Indigenous people for Halloween.

For a long time, mainstream schools celebrated Thanksgiving by having children make paper headdresses. Some students would dress as Indigenous people, while others would dress as Pilgrims. The class or school would act out the myth of the first Thanksgiving. Some still do this.

CHAPTER 3

How Is Cultural Appropriation Harmful?

Indigenous warriors hold a place of honor in Indigenous societies, yet their image has been one of the most exploited and misused in the dominant culture. Sports teams across the country have appropriated their likeness as mascots. Football, baseball, and basketball are some of the biggest sports in the country, and countless fans fill stadiums to watch professional, college, and even high school sports. Millions of people watch and cheer for their favorite teams. Reducing Indigenous warriors to cartoon character mascots insults and demeans Indigenous culture in front of huge audiences.

Indigenous protesters call on sports teams to change names and mascots.

This kind of appropriation has been a major source of trauma for Indigenous people in the United States. Mascots have little, if anything, to do with Indigenous peoples themselves and certainly do not represent them. Instead, mascots give a false sense of who Indigenous people are and show only stereotypes of Indigenous ways of life. They do nothing to honor the diversity of Indigenous cultures in the U.S. Mascots like the Braves, Chiefs, Indians, or even Savages can invoke an unhealthy association with Indigenous people, potentially depicting them as bloodthirsty and violent people.

The use of this imagery also gives a false sense of entitlement to fans. They start to believe that it is acceptable to attend games dressed in feathers or wearing red face paint. They refer to themselves as "Indians" and wear symbols that are considered sacred in Indigenous communities. Using Indigenous images as a mascot allows sports fans to take and remake pieces of Indigenous culture without consent or any historical knowledge. Those fans may never realize how harmful or traumatic their actions can be.

For decades, Cleveland's Major League Baseball team's logo was a harmful stereotype named "Chief Wahoo." The fans dressed up at games with fake war bonnets and painted their faces.

While some sports teams have changed their mascots, many more need to follow suit. Some teams have worked with Indigenous advisers and made important changes. Two professional teams that recently made this change are the **NFL**'s Washington Commanders and the **MLB**'s Cleveland Guardians. Both changed their team's name, mascot, and fan traditions. Local school boards are also moving in this direction. Many have voted to change mascots and team names that reference Indigenous imagery such as headdresses, tomahawks, and chiefs. Some states have even passed laws making it illegal for a school to have an offensive mascot.

Change the Mascot rallies have been held throughout the country.

CHAPTER 4

How Is Cultural Appropriation Different than Sharing Culture?

Cultural appropriation uses parts of a culture without permission. There are ways, however, to share cultural practices and knowledge without appropriation.

People in other cultures can learn from Indigenous groups and from community elders. Doing so demonstrates a genuine commitment to education and learning, which is not appropriation. Taking that knowledge without approval to make money from it is appropriation, though. People should honor and respect different cultures, and they should understand that they do not have ownership of that cultural knowledge.

In the 19th century, White writers collected stories from Indigenous elders, wrote them down, and then sold them. The White writers benefited financially from those stories, but the money they earned was not allocated or shared with the Indigenous people from which the material originated.

Dustin Beaulieu is a Dakota cultural educator. Here, he is teaching fourth graders Dakota values and language.

Later, those stories entered the public domain, meaning that it was now legal for anyone to use them. People retold the stories in textbooks and other types of publications. Still, the Indigenous cultures did not benefit. They also had no control over how their stories were used. In some Indigenous traditions, for example, Coyote is a trickster or troublemaker. In others, Coyote is a major sacred character with divine creative powers. White people confused the characters and stories and often retold them incorrectly.

Sharing culture can also be done by supporting Indigenous artists, writers, and craftspeople. Buying Indigenous jewelry, art, or blankets can reinforce Indigenous economies. Buying mass-produced jewelry, art, or blankets made to look Indigenous, however, is harmful appropriation, as someone else is making money from Indigenous cultures and traditions.

Indigenous artistry and beading is a time-honored practice.

Indigenous artisans often combine traditional and modern techniques and equipment.

To understand and appreciate someone else's culture, it must be entered from a place of self-awareness. When space is entered in such a way, people become more mindful of the space they are taking in respect to others. Instead of taking over another's identity, it can be celebrated and honored by simply learning about it. To ensure that a culture is being appreciated and not appropriated, seek out permission and question whether actions being made in relation to these other cultures are harmful or not.

Jane Johnston Schoolcraft

Jane Johnston was a poet and the first major Indigenous American woman writer in U.S. literature. Johnston was Scotch-Irish Ojibwe. Her mother was Ojibwe and her father was a fur trader. She lived with her family in Sault Ste. Marie, Michigan, where she spoke Ojibwe, English, and French.

Johnston married a U.S. Indian agent named Henry Rowe Schoolcraft. He was a White ethnographer. Johnston taught Schoolcraft the Ojibwe language, as well as translated Ojibwe stories and histories for him. He wrote down these Indigenous stories, traditions, and cultural practices.

Johnston wrote in both Ojibwe and English, and her poetry was filled with grief and loneliness. Two of her children died, while her remaining two children were sent away to boarding school against her wishes. Johnston died young, at the age of 42.

CHAPTER 5

How Can We Be Better?

There are healthy ways to use Indigenous words and phrases and respect Indigenous culture, but it is essential that Indigenous people be central participants in this conversation. Working with Indigenous communities is a great way to start.

We all come from different positions of **privilege**. There are also different types of privilege. Privilege is a special right or advantage that is only available to specific people or groups. It is not earned. In the United States, being White is a racial privilege. Other examples of privilege include being male or an English speaker. It is difficult to get ahead in a world that is not made for you, but we can use our own privilege to support and help those around us.

Think about Indigenous images you see in the place you live or the books you read. Who created the images? What is the purpose of the images?

Start with Yourself!

Everybody can do something. Just start somewhere and start small. Build your self-awareness and your knowledge in the following ways:

- Learn more about different Indigenous cultures and groups. Try to learn the differences between different Indigenous peoples, and do not lump them all together.

- Unlearn the stereotypes and historical myths told about Indigenous peoples. Reject cultural appropriation.

- Learn more about Indigenous history in the United States, including the facts surrounding the official policies of the government.

Be an Ally!

Being an ally is the first step in becoming a champion for racial justice work. Allies recognize their privilege, and they use it in solidarity with others. You can use your own privilege to demonstrate solidarity in the following ways:

- Call out cultural appropriation when you see it. If someone you know or love says something insensitive or dresses up as an Indigenous person for Halloween, you can be a good ally and let them know what they are doing is inappropriate. You can help to turn that moment into a learning moment.

- Support Indigenous creators, musicians, and athletes. Share their work with your friends and family.

- Continue to learn and be open to learning. You will make mistakes, and that is all right. Learn from those mistakes and use them to help you succeed in the future. You could help make a difference and allow someone to be seen and understood.

Be an Advocate!

Being an **advocate** goes beyond allyship. Advocates use their privilege to challenge supremacy. They are willing to be uncomfortable, to learn, and to stand up for equal rights. You can do the same by following these suggestions:

- Stand with Indigenous people to increase their representation. For example, talk to the principal and school board and encourage them to take steps to hire more Indigenous teachers.

- Stand united against historical myths that fuel hatred toward nondominant cultures. Ask your teachers to include Indigenous history in their classrooms, and make a list of books for others to read on related matters.

Think about what makes you who you are. What are some ways people can honor each other's differences?

Be an Activist!

Activists fight for both political and social change. They give up their own privileges and work together to fight against inequality. They understand that when one group suffers, all groups suffer. You can also become an activist for change in the following ways:

- Fight against anti-Indigenous policies and support Indigenous sovereignty.

- Look into Indigenous movements active today. Lead a class discussion about the movement, sharing the movement's goals and objectives.

Take the Challenge!

Read all the books in the Racial Justice in America series. Engage in the community of activism. Create a podcast, newsletter, video, or social media campaign and include a segment about cultural appropriation.

- Research examples of Indigenous cultural appropriation 100 years ago, 50 years ago, and today.

- Explain how each act of appropriation is harmful.

- Share positive steps that have taken place to right some of these wrongs. Also, share what still needs to be done.

Share your learning. Encourage others to learn more and to act upon what they've learned. Then, when you know more, do more.

Think about your school or local team mascots. Are there any harmful depictions that should be changed?

EXTEND YOUR LEARNING

BOOKS

Bell, Samantha. *Thanksgiving: The Making of a Myth*. Cherry Lake Publishing, Ann Arbor, MI, 2024.

Chambers, Catherine. *American Indian Stories and Legends*. Heinemann-Raintree, Chicago, 2014.

Loh-Hagan, Virgina. *Stand Up, Speak Out: Indigenous Rights*. 45th Parallel Press, Ann Arbor, MI, 2022.

O'Brien, Cynthia. *Encyclopedia of American Indian History and Culture: Stories, Timelines, Maps and More*. National Geographic Kids, Boone, IA, 2019.

WEBSITES

With an adult, learn more online with these suggested searches.

"National Museum of the American Indian." Smithsonian.

"What Is Cultural Appropriation?" PBS Learning Media.

GLOSSARY

advocate (AD-vuh-kuht) a person who uses their voice to support a cause

ally (A-lie) a person who supports a cause

colonization (kah-luh-nuh-ZAY-shuhn) the building of settlements on land belonging to others in order to increase a nation's power and/or wealth; often accomplished by armed force

consent (kuhn-SENT) explicit approval or agreement

cultural appropriation (KUHLCH-ruhl uh-proh-pree-AY-shuhn) mimicking or co-opting another person or group's identity in a harmful way

demeans (di-MEENS) treats as less than

derogatory (di-RAH-guh-tor-ee) harmful or belittling

dominant culture (DAH-muh-nuhnt KUHL-chuhr) a group that holds the most power and privilege in a society; includes language, religion, political representation, traditions, and worldviews

entitlement (in-TIE-tuhl-muhnt) having the immediate right to

ethnographer (eth-NAHG-ruh-fuhr) a person who studies and documents the culture of a particular group

federally recognized (FE-druhl-ee RE-kig-nyezd) legal status for Indigenous nations

genocide (JE-nuh-sied) the intentional destruction of a group of people

mascots (MA-skahts) a person, animal, or object representing a team

MLB (EM-EL-BEE) Major League Baseball

NFL (EN-EF-EL) National Football League

nondominant culture (NON-dah-muh-nuhnt KUHL-chuhr) a group or groups that hold less power and privilege in a society than the dominant culture; their language, religion, traditions, and worldviews are often overlooked, misrepresented, or belittled

privilege (PRIV-lij) a right granted to some, but not all, people

regalia (ri-GAYL-YUH) symbols that show status; ceremonial dress

sovereignty (SAH-vruhn-tee) independence to self-govern

stereotypes (STAIR-ee-uh-tieps) an idea many people have about a thing that is usually untrue

trauma (TRAH-muh) intense mental or emotional harm

INDEX